How to use this book

Follow the advice, in italics, given for you on each page.
Support the children as they read the text that is shaded in cream.
Praise *the children at every step!*

Detailed guidance is provided in the Read Write Inc. Phonics Handbook

9 reading activities

Children:
Practise reading the speed sounds.
Read the green, red and challenge words for the story.
Listen as you read the introduction.
Discuss the vocabulary check with you.
Read the story.
Re-read the story and discuss the 'questions to talk about'.
Read the story with fluency and expression.
Answer the questions to 'read and answer'.
Practise reading the speed words.

Speed sounds

Consonants   *Say the pure sounds (do not add 'uh').*

f ff ph	l ll le	m mm	n nn kn	r rr wr	s ss se (c) ce	v ve	z zz s	sh	th	ng nk

b bb	c k ck	d dd	g gg (gu)	h	j g ge	p pp	(qu)	t tt	w (wh)	x	y	ch tch

Vowels   *Say the sounds in and out of order.*

at	hen head	in	on	up	day make	see tea happy he	high smile lie find	blow home no

zoo brute blue	look	car	for door snore	fair care	whirl nurse letter	shout	boy spoil

*Each box contains one sound but sometimes more than one grapheme. Focus graphemes are **circled**.*

Green words

dark   steal   hard   ate   strong   sh ook   free

night   sight   light   fright   high

shine   while   hide   white   pile   pine   fine   nice   prize   nine   twice

quite   time   life   like   kite   wide   smile   five   rice   pie   lie

al`ways   chil`dren   stor`y   light`ning

in`side   be`side

animal   →   animals   ask   →   asked   look   →   looking

peep   →   peeped   untie   →   untied   whine   →   whined

decide   →   decided   glide   →   gliding   guide   →   guided

fry   →   fried   spice   →   spicy   wife   →   wives

slice   → slices

all   who   h<u>er</u>   <u>there</u>   <u>their</u>   c<u>oul</u>d   Humans

A box full of light

Introduction

Just imagine if there was no sunshine and it was always dark. What would it be like to live in such a place?

In this story, in the Land of Animals, it is always dark. Fox has heard that in the Land of Humans there is a bright light. He decides to go and search for it with his friend, Kestrel. Flashes of lightning lead them to a camp. They discover a big box and steal it in the night.

What will be in the box?
Will Fox and Kestrel have stolen the light?

Story written by Gill Munton
Illustrated by Tim Archbold

Vocabulary check

Discuss the meaning (as used in the story) after the children have read each word.

	definition:	sentence/phrase:
whined	a moany, grumpy voice	'I don't like this at all!' whined Fox.
pal	friend	I need a good pal to help me.
humans	people: men, women and children	In the land of Humans.
gliding	flying smoothly	Kestrel gliding on her wide grey wings...
trotted	gentle running	while Fox trotted along the track.
guided	led	The light guided them to a camp.
chink	hole	Kestrel spotted a chink in the box.
what a prize	what a great thing to have	Then we'll grab the box of light. What a prize!
bolt of light	a line of light, like lightning	A bolt of white light shot up.

Punctuation to note in this story:
1. Capital letters to start sentences and full stops to end sentences
2. Capital letters for names
3. Exclamation marks to show anger, shock and surprise
4. 'Wait and see' dots ...
5. Apostrophe to show contractions: can't

A box full of light

A long time ago, in the Land of the Animals,

it was *always* night.

It was quite dark, all the time.

The animals had a hard life,

as they kept bumping into things.

"I don't like this at all!" whined Fox.

"I can't see to find my lunch."

"What I need," he said to himself,

"is a good pal, to help me.

But who shall I pick?"

In the end he decided on Kestrel, with her strong wings and her good sight.

The next day, Kestrel said to Fox,
"In the Land of Humans, there is
a bright light. Kite told me. Shall we go
and steal it?"

So off they went,
Kestrel gliding on her wide grey wings
while Fox trotted along the track.

Twice, they saw bright flashes of lightning.

"That must be the light!" said Fox with a smile.

The light guided them to a camp with five tents.

Men cooked fish with spicy fried rice,

and their wives and children ate slices of rabbit pie.

It was a fine sight.

"That smells nice!" said Kestrel.

"This must be the Land of

Humans."

Fox was looking at a big box,

almost hidden behind a pile of pine logs.

"What's inside it, do you think?" he asked.

Kestrel spotted a chink in the box.

"I think it might be – the light!" she said.

"Let's hide until the men go to sleep," said Fox.

"We can lie behind that pile of logs.

Then we'll grab the box of light.

What a prize!"

And that is what they did.

On the way back, Kestrel had to rest for a while.

Fox sat beside the box as she slept.

He kept looking at the box.

He sniffed the lid.

He untied the lid and peeped into the box –

but the lid slipped right off,

and a bolt of white light shot up, up,

into the blackness of the night!

Fox had such a fright that he shook Kestrel's wing until she sat up.

"Fetch the light back!" he said.

So Kestrel took a long flight –

nine, ten, eleven miles -

so high that she went right out of sight.

But she didn't catch the bright light.

* * * * * * * * * * * * * * * * * *

This story has a happy ending.

The bright light was the Sun!

Fox had set it free, and it stayed high up

so that it could shine on all the animals as well as on Humans.

Questions to talk about

Re-read the page. Read the question to the children. Tell them whether it is a **FIND IT** *question or* **PROVE IT** *question.*

FIND IT

✓ *Turn to the page*

✓ *Read the question*

✓ *Find the answer*

PROVE IT

✓ *Turn to the page*

✓ *Read the question*

✓ *Find your evidence*

✓ *Explain why*

Page 9:	FIND IT	*Why did the animals not like being in the dark all the time?*
Page 10:	FIND IT	*Why did Fox choose Kestrel to help him?*
Page 11:	FIND IT	*What was their plan?*
Page 12:	FIND IT	*Where did the light take them? What did Fox find?*
Page 13:	FIND IT	*What was the next part of the plan'?*
Page 14:	PROVE IT	*Why did Fox keep looking at the box?* *What happened when the lid slipped off the box?*
Page 15:	PROVE IT	*Why couldn't Kestrel catch the light?*

Questions to read and answer

(Children complete without your help.)

1. Why was Fox fed up?

2. What did Fox and Kestrel want to steal from the Land of Humans?

3. How did Kestrel know the light was in the box?

4. What happened when Fox untied the lid of the box?

5. Were Fox and Kestrel right to steal the light? Explain.

Speed words

Children practise reading the words across the rows, down the columns and in and out of order clearly and quickly.

children	peeped	lightning	animals	always
high	while	decided	nice	time
beside	fine	ago	behind	saw
someone	almost	anyone	how	now